THE MONSTER HEALTH BOOK

A Guide to Eating Healthy, Being Active & Feeling Great for Monsters & Kids!

Edward Miller

Holiday House / New York

Yogurt

Mixed Nuts

This book is useful to read when you're looking for something good to eat, when you're helping in the kitchen, and when you're at the supermarket. It will help you make good food choices.

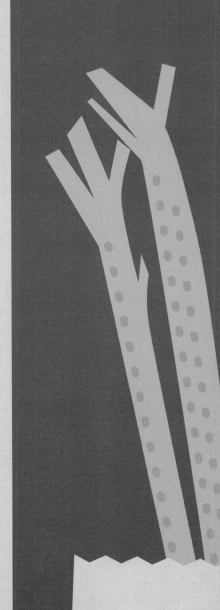

Many thanks to Lisa Sasson, Clinical Assistant Professor of Nutrition, Food Studies, and Public Health at New York University, and to Marilyn Tanner, American Dietetic Association Spokesperson, Pediatric Dietician at St. Louis Children's Hospital, and study coordinator at Washington University School of Medicine, for their expert knowledge on nutrition; and to Donna Byrne, Physical Education teacher, Old Saybrook Middle School, for her expert knowledge on fitness.—E. M.

Library of Congress Cataloging-in-Publication Data
Miller, Edward, 1964-
The monster health book : a guide to eating healthy, being active & feeling great for monsters & kids!
/ by Edward Miller.
    p. cm.
  ISBN-10: 0-8234-1956-8 (hardcover)
  ISBN-13: 978-0-8234-1956-2 (hardcover)
1. Nutrition—Juvenile literature. 2. Health—Juvenile literature. I. Title.

RA784.M4894 2006
613.7—dc22   2005046383

CONTENTS

LUXE!

SODA!

SUPER COMBO!

all you can eat!

GET MORE FREE!

IT'S ALIVE!

EAT WELL, BE WELL

Monsters live on food. Food is filled with nutrients—the good things in food—that keep them breathing, thinking, moving, and growing. Just like us, monsters need food to do all the tasks they can do, such as running and jumping.

But how do monsters know what foods are healthy to eat and how much is enough? With signs that say to "super size," it's hard for them to make wise decisions. With help from nutritionists, who study how foods affect the body, and the United States Department of Agriculture (USDA), which recommends ways to eat healthy, monsters can make better choices, and so can we. Let's begin with the food groups.

THE 5 FOOD GROUPS

Food comes from all over. Some comes from animals, such as milk from cows and eggs from chickens. Some foods grow on trees, such as apples and oranges. Lettuce and carrots grow in the ground, while grapes and melons grow on vines. A lot of tasty foods come from the ocean, such as fish, shrimp, and clams.

Foods are placed into five major groups to help us to identify them: vegetable group, fruit group, meat and bean group, whole grain group, and milk group.

1. VEGETABLE GROUP

Vegetables are plants with edible parts. They have many nutrients in them that are good for you. You should eat 2 to 3 cups of vegetables a day. A cup is about the size of a baseball. It's important to eat a mix of vegetables, including green and orange ones.

Broccoli
People have eaten broccoli for more than 2,000 years. Roman soldiers ate broccoli.

Onions
During the Middle Ages, onions were so valuable that people paid their rent with them.

Cucumbers
Inside a cucumber it can be up to 20 degrees cooler than the temperature outside.

Tomatoes
Tomatoes were once thought to be poisonous.

Celery
You use more energy to eat and digest celery than the celery provides.

Lettuce
Ancient Greeks thought eating lettuce made you sleepy.

Collard Greens
According to folklore, hanging a collard leaf over a doorway will ward off evil spirits.

Zucchini
Zucchini can grow to several feet long in a few weeks.

Peppers
Peppers can be green, red, yellow, orange, or purple.

Potatoes
Potatoes are the №1 vegetable in the U.S.

String Beans
String beans were first grown in Mexico more than 7,000 years ago.

Spinach
The cartoon character Popeye eats spinach because it contains iron, a mineral that gives you strength.

Carrots
The world record for the longest carrot is 16 feet 10½ inches.

2. FRUIT GROUP

Fruits are foods that come from trees and vines. They have many nutrients that make your body healthy. You should have $1\frac{1}{2}$ to 2 cups of fruit a day. A small apple is about $\frac{1}{2}$ cup. It's good to eat a variety of fruits so you get all the important nutrients your body needs.

Why did the orange stop rolling?

Because it was out of juice!

What do you call strawberries when they are sad?

Blueberries!

Strawberries
There is an old tale that says if you share a double strawberry with someone, you'll fall in love with him or her.

Pineapples
European explorers named this fruit pineapple because it looked like a pinecone with the flesh of an apple.

Mangoes
In India it's believed that the mango tree can grant wishes.

Plums
The Japanese plum is actually from China.

Pears
Pear trees can be as old as 100 years.

Grapes
Grapes are one of the oldest fruits, dating back 2,000 years. Spanish explorers brought them to the New World about 300 years ago.

Melons
Christopher Columbus brought melon seeds to the New World from Europe.

Watermelons
A watermelon is not a melon; it's a very large berry.

100% ORANGE JUICE

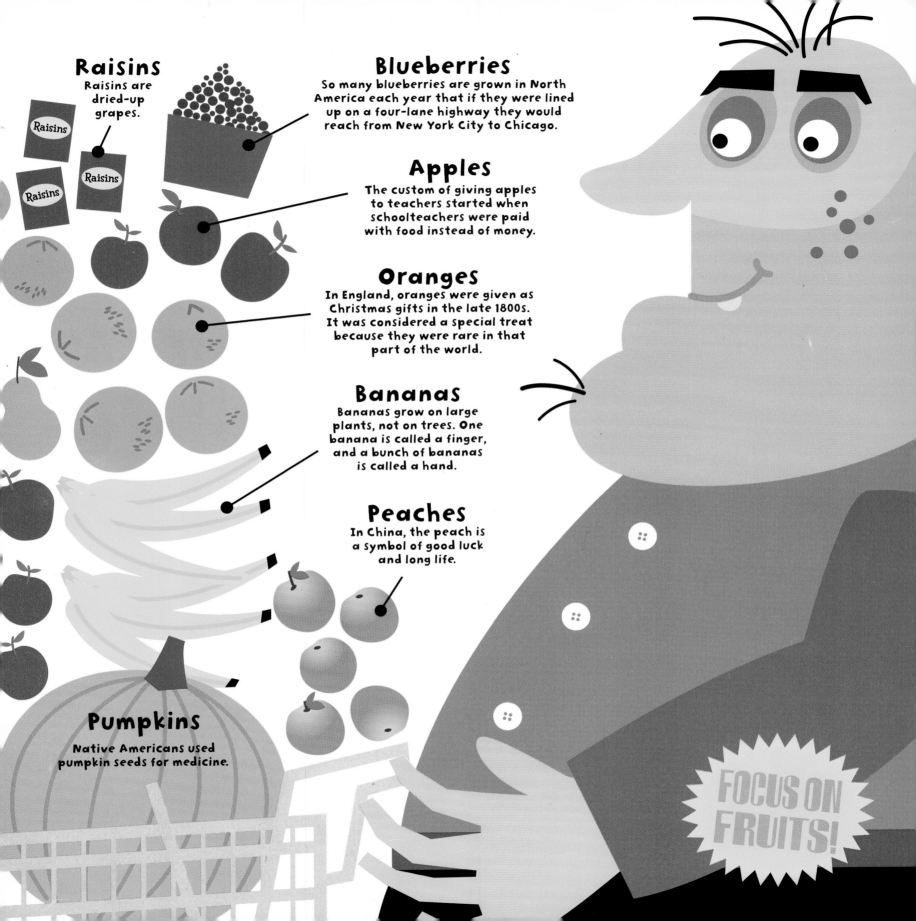

Raisins
Raisins are dried-up grapes.

Blueberries
So many blueberries are grown in North America each year that if they were lined up on a four-lane highway they would reach from New York City to Chicago.

Apples
The custom of giving apples to teachers started when schoolteachers were paid with food instead of money.

Oranges
In England, oranges were given as Christmas gifts in the late 1800s. It was considered a special treat because they were rare in that part of the world.

Bananas
Bananas grow on large plants, not on trees. One banana is called a finger, and a bunch of bananas is called a hand.

Peaches
In China, the peach is a symbol of good luck and long life.

Pumpkins
Native Americans used pumpkin seeds for medicine.

FOCUS ON FRUITS!

3. MEAT AND BEAN GROUP

Meats, beans, nuts, and fish are in the same group because they have many of the same nutrients. You should have 4 to 6 ounces of items from this food group a day. An egg is about 1 ounce. A hamburger is about 3 ounces. It's best to boil, grill, or roast meat instead of fry it in fatty cooking oil.

HAMBURGERS

It's believed that the first hamburger was sold at the St. Louis World's Fair in 1904.

STEAKS

During the War of 1812, a butler named Sam Wilson shipped meat stamped U.S. beef to the soldiers. The soldiers nicknamed this beef "Uncle Sam's beef." The Uncle Sam character has become an American patriotic symbol.

EGGS

The average chicken can lay 255 eggs a year. That's about 21 eggs a month.

CHICKEN

There are more chickens than people on Earth.

TOFU

Chinese legend says that tofu was invented by an ancient Chinese prince who tried to create a recipe that would make him immortal.

FISH

Fish have been on Earth for more than 500 million years. There are more than 250,000 different kinds.

TURKEY

The National Turkey Federation has given a turkey to the president of the United States every Thanksgiving since 1941. After the ceremony, the turkey is retired to a farm instead of cooked.

HAMBURGERS

STEAKS

CHICKEN ON SALE!

PEANUT BUTTER

It takes around 550 peanuts to make a 12-ounce jar of peanut butter.

MIXED NUTS

Nuts include peanuts, almonds, cashews, pecans, walnuts, pistachios, and many other varieties. Former U.S. Presidents Thomas Jefferson and Jimmy Carter were both peanut farmers.

PEAS

In England the correct way to eat peas is to squash them with a fork. Peas are in this group because they are seeds.

GO LEAN ON PROTEIN!

BEANS

The ancient Greeks and Romans used beans for voting. Black beans were no votes and white beans were yes votes.

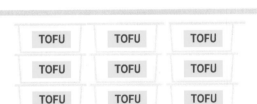

NOT-so-healthy, too-fatty meats:

- meat with fat you can see
- hot dog
- sausage
- bologna
- bacon

4. WHOLE GRAIN GROUP

WHOLE GRAIN BREAD	TORTILLAS
WHOLE GRAIN CEREAL	POPCORN
OATMEAL	CORN
BROWN RICE	

Grains are seeds from plants. Your body needs the fiber and nutrients found in grains to stay healthy. It's important to eat foods that are made from whole seeds, so choose foods that say "whole grain" on the package. It's good to eat 3 to 3½ ounces from the whole grain group a day. One slice of bread is about 1 ounce. A ½ cup of cooked rice or noodles is also about 1 ounce.

Make half your grains whole!

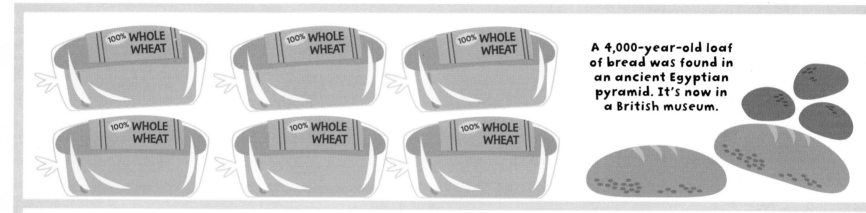

A 4,000-year-old loaf of bread was found in an ancient Egyptian pyramid. It's now in a British museum.

January is Oatmeal Month. More oatmeal is sold in January than in any other month.

Tortillas are a popular Mexican food made from corn or wheat grains.

An ear of corn has about 800 kernels in 16 rows.

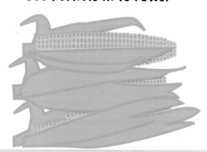

Other whole grains:

- whole grain barley
- buckwheat
- whole rye
- wild rice
- sorghum
- quinoa
- bulgur
- millet

WHOLE GRAIN *DELICIOUS!* **WHEAT CEREAL**

Some boxed cereals are packed with vitamins, but may also have a lot of sugar and not much fiber, so read labels and choose wisely.

WHOLE GRAIN *DELICIOUS!* **WHEAT CEREAL**

Whole Grain *Tasty!* **Bran Flakes**

NOT-so-healthy grain foods that have less nutritional value because they're made with only part of the grain:

- white bread
- pizza crust
- bagels
- pasta
- graham crackers
- crackers
- pretzels

Rice is grown on every continent except Antarctica, where it is too cold.

BROWN RICE · BROWN RICE · BROWN RICE

Brigg's **CORN FLAKES** WHOLE GRAIN

WHOLE GRAIN *DELICIOUS!* **WHEAT CEREAL**

Whole Grain *Tasty!* **Bran Flakes**

Whole Grain **Raisin Bran** *Nutritious!*

National Popcorn Day is January 19. Hold the butter and salt.

POPCORN · POPCORN · POPCORN · POPCORN

Brigg's **CORN FLAKES** WHOLE GRAIN

WHOLE GRAIN *DELICIOUS!* **WHEAT CEREAL**

Whole Grain *Tasty!* **Bran Flakes**

Whole Grain **Raisin Bran** *Nutritious!*

POPCORN · POPCORN · POPCORN · POPCORN · POPCORN · POPCORN

Brigg's **CORN FLAKES** WHOLE GRAIN

WHOLE GRAIN *DELICIOUS!* **WHEAT CEREAL**

Whole Grain *Tasty!* **Bran Flakes**

Whole Grain **Raisin Bran**

5. MILK GROUP

Milk products are foods made from cow's milk. Milk has vitamins and minerals that help build strong teeth and bones. Low-fat and fat-free milk products are the best choices. You should have 2 to 3 cups from the milk group a day.

Milk

It takes about 350 squirts from a cow to get a gallon of milk.

Almost every American family had its own cow in the 1850s.

Yogurt

Americans eat more than 300,000 tons of yogurt a year.

Cheese

Cheese comes from a substance called curd. Curd, found in milk, settles to the bottom of the liquid.

There are many kinds of cheeses, including American, Swiss, cheddar, mozzarella, Parmesan, and cottage cheese. Low-fat varieties of these cheeses are better for you.

Some people can't drink milk because it contains an ingredient called lactose that upsets their stomachs. They can drink lactose-free or soy milk instead.

THE FOOD PYRAMID

The United States Department of Agriculture (USDA) recommends how much we should eat from each food group to stay healthy. The amounts of food are determined by your age, whether you are a boy or a girl, and your activity level.

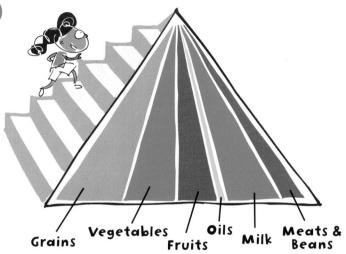

Grains Vegetables Fruits Oils Milk Meats & Beans

OILS: LIQUID FAT

Although oils are not a food group, they are included in the food pyramid because they are essential for good health. Oils are fats that at room temperature are liquid. They are found in many foods. Fat stores energy for when you need it, helps you grow, keeps you warm, protects your bones from injury, helps your brain think, and keeps your skin healthy. But too much fat can make you overweight and clog your arteries. Foods that are low-fat and nonfat are the best choices. Three teaspoons (20 grams) a day are plenty.

Healthy fats:
- polyunsaturated
- monounsaturated

NOT-so-healthy fats:
- saturated
- trans fat

Healthy fatty foods:
- nuts
- seeds
- peanut butter
- olive oil
- low-fat cheeses

NOT-so-healthy fatty foods:
- fried foods
- bacon
- salad dressings
- whole milk
- butter
- cheese
- mayonnaise
- bologna

YOU ARE WHAT YOU EAT:
NUTRIENTS IN FOODS

Nutrients are the good things found in foods that make your body strong and healthy. Eating a variety of items from all the food groups will help you get all the nutrients your body craves.

Vitamins

There are 13 major vitamins, and they are found in foods. They do many good things for your body. Some help make strong bones; others help your body use energy, heal cuts and scrapes, keep gums healthy, make blood, and help your eyes to see.

B3 B6

Vitamin A
helps your eyes to see.
Found in carrots and milk.

Vitamin C
helps scrapes to heal.
Found in oranges.

B5

B12

B2

Folic Acid

Biotin

Vitamin E
builds strong cells. Found in eggs and peanut butter.

K B1

Sugar

found in fruits is good for you because it gives your body energy. But refined sugar added to candy, cakes, cookies, fruit drinks, and other sweets is not good because too much can slow you down.

Water is necessary for all body functions. It carries nutrients to your cells, and it helps to control your body's temperature and to remove waste when you urinate. It's important to drink 5 to 6 glasses of water a day.

A person can live only one week without water.

A cow drinks enough water each day to fill a bathtub.

Carbohydrates

are nutrients in foods that give your body energy.

Good sources of carbohydrates:
- whole grain breads and cereals
- potatoes

Proteins

are nutrients in foods that help build muscle and bones, and make your toenails and fingernails strong, your skin healthy, and your hair shiny and healthy.

Good sources of protein:
- meats
- nuts
- vegetables
- beans

Fiber

is the material in food that cannot be used by the body. Fiber cleans out your intestines and makes it easier for you to go to the bathroom.

Good sources of fiber:
- whole grain breads and cereals
- fruits and vegetables

Salt (sodium) keeps your body's water and blood in good shape. One teaspoon a day is enough.

Salt

Minerals

are elements found in the earth and water that are good for your body. Some minerals help make your bones and teeth strong; others help your lungs to breathe, your blood to clot, your heart to beat, and your other muscles to move, too.

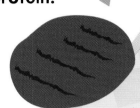

Potassium helps your heart beat and muscles move. Found in meat, bananas, and potatoes.

Copper

Magnesium

Molybdenum

Phosphorus

Calcium builds strong teeth and bones. Found in milk and leafy green vegetables.

Selenium

Zinc

Iron helps blood carry oxygen through your body. Found in spinach, red meat, and eggs.

Iodine

Manganese

Chromium

Fluoride protects teeth from decay. Found in water.

IN THE KITCHEN:
COUNTING & LABELS

Counting Calories

The amount of energy in food is measured in calories.

1 medium carrot = 26 calories
1 medium apple = 60 calories
1 cup of skim milk = 80 calories
¾ cup of whole grain wheat cereal = 100 calories
2 scrambled eggs = 150 calories
1 chicken leg (without skin) = 180 calories

The USDA recommends how many calories an active kid should eat each day to maintain a healthy weight.

Girls	Calories
ages 4 to 8	1,400 to 1,800
ages 9 to 13	1,800 to 2,200

Boys	Calories
ages 4 to 8	1,600 to 2,000
ages 9 to 13	2,000 to 2,600

Food is measured in grams, a metric unit of weight.
1 gram (g.) = 15½ grains of rice = the mass of a paper clip
1 gram (g.) = 1000 milligrams (mg.)
6 grams = 1 teaspoon (tsp.)

Nutrition Facts Labels

On many food products there is a Nutrition Facts label. It lists the nutrients and ingredients in the product. The list helps you plan a healthy meal by selecting foods that are nutritious.

① The serving size tells you how much is in a serving and how many servings are in the container. Use this information to figure out how many servings you are eating.

② The amount per serving tells you how many calories are in each serving and how many calories come from fat. If you eat two servings, you'll be eating twice the number of calories listed on the box.

③ Use this information to help limit these nutrients in your diet. If you eat 2,000 calories each day you should eat fewer than 65 grams of total fat, 20 grams of saturated fat, 300 milligrams of cholesterol, and 2,400 milligrams of sodium.

④ Use this information to make sure you get all the nutrients you need.

⑤ The daily values can help you figure out if you're getting too much or too little of each nutrient. The daily values are based on a 2,000-calorie diet for adults but give an idea of what most people need.

⑥ The list of ingredients tells you what is in the food. The main ingredients are listed first. This information is especially important to kids with food allergies.

milk

100% FAT FREE

ONE-HALF GALLON
SKIM MILK

Nutrition Facts
Serving Size 1 cup (240mL)
Servings per Container 8

Amount Per Serving

Calories 80	Calories from Fat 0
	% Daily Value
Total Fat 0g	0%
Saturated Fat 0g	0%
Cholesterol 3mg	1%
Sodium 130 mg	5%
Carbohydrate 12g	4%
Dietary Fiber 0g	0%
Sugars 12g	
Protein 8g	16%
Vitamin A 10%	Vitamin C 2%
Calcium 30%	Iron 0%
Vitamin D 25%	

• Percent Daily Values are based on a 2,000 calorie diet. Your daily values may be higher or lower depending on your calorie needs.

INGREDIENTS: SKIM MILK, VITAMIN A PALMITATE, VITAMIN D₃

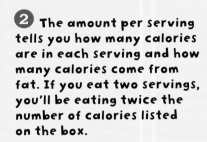

WHOLE GRAIN WHEAT CEREAL

Nutrition Facts

Serving Size 3/4 cup (30g)
Servings Per Container About 12

Amount Per Serving

Calories	110
Calories from Fat	10

	% Daily Value
Total Fat 1g	1%
Saturated Fat 0mg	0%
Trans Fat 0mg	0%
Polyunsaturated Fat 0mg	0%
Monounsaturated Fat 0mg	0%
Cholesterol 0mg	0%
Sodium 190mg	9%
Potassium 90mg	3%
Total Carbohydrate 23g	8%
Dietary Fiber 3g	10%
Sugars 5g	
Other Carbohydrate 15g	
Protein 2g	
Vitamin A	10%
Vitamin C	100%
Calcium	100%
Iron	100%
Vitamin D	10%
Vitamin E	100%
Vitamin B₆	100%
Folic Acid	100%
Vitamin B₁₂	100%
Phosphorus	7%
Magnesium	8%
Zinc	100%
Copper	5%

• Percent Daily Values are based on a 2,000 calorie diet. Your daily values may be higher or lower depending on your calorie needs.

INGREDIENTS: WHOLE GRAIN WHEAT, SUGAR, CALCIUM, CARBONATE, WHOLE GRAIN BROWN RICE, CORN SYRUP, SALT, CORN BRAN, LACTOSE, DISTILLED MONOGLYCERIDES, ANNATTO EXTRACT COLOR, ZINC, VITAMIN C, IRON, VITAMIN E, VITAMIN B₆, VITAMIN B₂, VITAMIN B₁, FOLIC ACID, VITAMIN B₁₂, VITAMIN A, VITAMIN D.

BREAK FOR BREAKFAST:
START THE DAY OFF RIGHT

Eating breakfast is a very smart thing to do! Why? Because your body and mind need to regain their energy after a night's sleep. Your body won't run without fuel just as a car won't run without gas.

It's a fact that kids who eat breakfast do better in school because they're energized and ready to learn, think, and be creative. Kids who skip breakfast are more likely to be overweight and tired because they eat more junk food during the day—studies prove it!

Some healthy breakfast choices:

- egg omelet with vegetables and orange or grapefruit juice
- whole grain toast with apple butter and a piece of fruit or fresh fruit cup
- whole grain cereal, skim milk, and fruit
- French toast made with whole grain bread with fruit and maple syrup
- pancakes made with whole grain flour with blueberries
- low-fat yogurt with fruit

Some NOT-so-healthy breakfast choices:

- bacon and sausage
- white toast with butter and jelly
- donuts, cookies, cakes, and pastries
- sugary cereals with whole milk
- French toast, pancakes, and waffles with butter, syrup, or whipped cream
- juice drinks or soda
- fried potatoes, french fries, and hash browns

No Time for Breakfast?

Here are some helpful tips to make time—*it's that important!*

- Set your alarm clock 10 minutes earlier.
- Set the kitchen table the night before.
- Pack your lunch and school bag the night before.
- Plan your breakfast menu the night before.
- Plan your outfit the night before.

Breakfast on the run!

Some kids just don't feel that hungry in the morning. If that's you, start with something light, such as a piece of fruit and a glass of skim milk. On the way to school have a cereal bar or a small muffin. Your stomach will thank you for it. Avoid having a late-night snack so you're more likely to be hungry in the morning.

Some schools serve breakfast before classes. Breakfast time at school is a great time to talk with friends, study for a quiz, discuss projects, and get the fuel you need—all at the same time.

WHOLE GRAIN DELICIOUS! WHEAT CEREAL

LUNCHTIME: TIME TO REFUEL

So what will it be? Will you bring your lunch or buy it at the school cafeteria? See what's in the refrigerator and what's on the school cafeteria menu and discuss with your parents what you would like for lunch. Remember, if you choose foods from all the food groups you'll be sure to get a nutritious lunch.

Some healthy lunch choices:

- grilled chicken sandwich
- turkey on whole wheat bread with light mayonnaise
- whole wheat pizza with peppers, mushrooms, or spinach
- peanut butter sandwich on whole wheat bread
- vegetable, pea, lentil, or bean soup
- baked potato or salad with light dressing
- nonfat or low-fat frozen yogurt
- low-fat milk
- fruit

Some NOT-so-healthy lunch choices:

- fried chicken or fish sandwich
- ham or bologna on white bread with cheese
- pizza with extra cheese, sausage, and pepperoni
- potato chips or cheese tortilla chips
- sodas, fruit punch, and fruit ades
- cookies, cakes, and candy
- chocolate whole milk
- hamburger
- french fries
- ice cream

Mustard and Ketchup have a lot of salt in them. Use them sparingly.

LUNCH SPECIAL!
Grilled Chicken with Salad and Carrots

The average American Kid will eat 1,500 peanut butter and jelly sandwiches before he or she graduates from high school.

Vending machines are filled with snacks and drinks that have lots of sugar. Choose items wisely.

Pack-a-Lunch Tips

• Pack your lunch in a lunch box or insulated lunch bag.

• It's best *not* to trade foods in your lunch box. You might be trading a nutritious food for something less healthy.

The sandwich is believed to have been invented by John Montague, the fourth Earl of Sandwich, England, in 1762. He ordered meat and cheese between 2 slices of bread so he could eat and play cards at the same time.

MUNCH TIME: HEALTHY SNACKS

Snacks are a good thing—they keep your body energized and growing. However, what you eat and when you eat are also important. It's a good idea to choose a snack from a food group you haven't had much of that day so that you'll get any missing nutrients your body is craving. Have a snack one to two hours before dinner. It will give you the energy you need without spoiling your dinner.

Healthy snacks:

- fruit
- oatmeal cookie
- whole grain toast with peanut butter
- carrot and celery sticks
- cherry tomatoes and cucumber slices
- trail mix (cereal, raisins, nuts)
- plain popcorn
- 100 percent fruit Popsicle
- low-fat frozen yogurt
- low-fat cheese sticks or cubes
- dried apricots, apples, and prunes

Snacks for special occasions (because they are not very nutritious):

- potato chips
- candy bars
- sugary cookies
- cake
- ice cream
- sugary candy
- fruit roll-ups
- donuts and pastries
- popcorn with butter and salt
- soda or fruit drinks with sugar

Snacks can be fun to make and decorate—be creative!

Lollipops were named after a racehorse named Lolly Pop in 1908.

A sweet treat for cavemen was honey from beehives.

Kids who spend more time watching TV and playing computer games tend to weigh more then kids who play outside. Why? Because kids who aren't active tend to eat more snacks and burn up fewer calories.

Hard candy is made from melting sugar in water. A high temperature makes hard candy and a low temperature makes chewy candy.

SWEET TOOTH: SWEETS

Sweets are products made with lots of sugar, such as candy, cookies, cakes, chocolate, ice cream, chewing gum, and soda. Although sugar tastes good, it has very few nutrients. If you eat too much of it and don't get enough exercise, you can become overweight. It can also harm your teeth. Eat sweets sparingly, no more than 8 teaspoons (48 grams) a day.

Other names for sugar:

- corn sweetener
- corn syrup
- fructose
- fruit juice concentrate
- glucose
- honey
- maltose
- molasses
- sucrose

Healthy Teeth & Gums

Food can stick, stain, and get caught between teeth—which can lead to tooth decay. Sugar, in particular, sticks to teeth and causes cavities. The way to healthy teeth and gums is through brushing and flossing. Fluoride in toothpaste and water helps protect your teeth.

- Brush your teeth twice a day with a soft bristle toothbrush.
- Floss between your teeth once a day.
- Replace your toothbrush every 3 months.
- Visit your dentist twice a year.
- Don't consume too many foods or drinks with sugar in them.
- Rinse your mouth with water after you eat sweets and chewy fruits.

Sweet Tooth

Toothpaste with Fluoride

25

DINNER IS SERVED!
SIT-DOWN DINNERS & FAST FOOD

Sit-down dinners have many benefits. If you sit down to dinner, you're more likely to have a nutritious meal than if you grab something and run off to practice, meet up with friends, or eat in front of the TV. It's often hard to make time for dinner with a family's busy schedule, but more and more families are trying to do so at least a few days a week.

Most people enjoy fast food once in a while, but eating it too often isn't healthy for you. Fast foods have a lot of fat, cholesterol, salt, and chemicals. Cut down on fat and calories by ordering grilled instead of fried foods, don't super size, and choose low-fat foods, such as low-fat cheese and milk.

Most nutritionists recommend not to eat fast food more than once a month.

Studies show that kids who eat dinner with their families are happier because they share more with one another.

There are more than 650,000 restaurants in the United States.

THE SKINNY ON FAT:
ILLNESSES, ALLERGIES & DISORDERS

To *be* healthy you need to *eat* healthy. If you eat lots of junk food and don't get enough nutrients, if you eat too much and aren't active, or if you don't eat enough for your body to function properly, it can lead to poor health.

Being Overweight

When someone has more body fat than is healthy, he or she is overweight. Someone who is very fat is called obese.

A kid can be overweight because of family genes. Genes are physical traits common to a family, such as hair color, height, and weight. Most kids, however, are overweight because of poor diet and not enough activity. If you eat a lot you need to exercise a lot too.

How do you know if you're the right weight? It depends on your age, height, body type, and whether you're a boy or a girl. Your doctor can tell you which weight range is right for you, using a chart called the Body Mass Index (BMI).

It's a mistake to compare your weight to that of your friends and classmates. The right weight for them may not be the right weight for you.

Diabetes

When your body is unable to change food into fuel or use the fuel effectively, you have an illness called diabetes. Like a car without fuel, your body starts to shut down. Kids with diabetes take a medicine called insulin. Someone who is overweight and isn't active is more likely to get diabetes.

High Blood Pressure

When your doctor wraps that cuff around your arm and pumps it up with air, he or she is checking your blood pressure. High blood pressure means that your heart is pumping blood too hard into your veins, causing pressure on the veins and heart. High blood pressure can be caused by being overweight and by eating too many salty foods.

High Cholesterol

Cholesterol is a fatty substance that helps you digest. But too much of this substance can build up inside your arteries causing them to clog and slow down the amount of blood flowing to your heart. Eating foods with a lot of fat can cause high cholesterol.

There's good news!

You can help prevent these illnesses from happening if you start taking care of your body now. Eat right, be active, and maintain a healthy weight. Have a heart—be good to your body!

Food Allergies

If your body reacts badly after eating something, you might have an allergy to that particular food. Some signs of food allergies are difficulty breathing, skin rash, or a swollen tongue and throat. The only solution is to avoid eating that food ever again. It's especially important for kids with allergies to read food labels, not to trade lunches, and to keep medication handy in case they have another allergic reaction.

Some common food allergies:

- milk
- nuts
- eggs
- wheat
- fish
- shellfish

Eating Disorders

Some young people have a fear of being fat. When someone has difficulty eating because of this fear, he or she has an eating disorder. Kids with disorders might go without eating or vomit up food after they eat. These kids become so thin it's unhealthy for them. Eating disorders often happen to girls and boys who believe they need to be thin to be liked.

Other boys think they need to be muscular to be accepted. These boys might take steroids, a family of drugs that makes muscles grow big and fast. Steroids can be very harmful.

An eating disorder is a very serious health condition that needs to be treated by a doctor.

EATING IS A BIG PART OF LIFE—MAKE IT A POSITIVE, FUN, AND HEALTHY EXPERIENCE!

SWEAT IT OUT!
THE IMPORTANCE OF BEING ACTIVE

Eating right is just one part of being healthy; the other part is physical fitness. Being physically fit means your body is strong, flexible, energized, and growing. You become physically fit by being active and using all your muscles every day. Kids should be active for at least 1 hour every day.

Your body will use up as many calories as it needs to in order to complete a task. It uses up hundreds of calories just to keep your heart and lungs working. To stay at the same weight you must use up the calories you eat each day. If you don't, you will gain weight.

Aerobic activities, such as jumping rope, running, and swimming, improve your breathing and get your heart pumping.

Strength activities, such as biking, dancing, and playing on the jungle gym, work your muscles.

Your body uses up:

- ½ calorie per minute sleeping
- 1 calorie per minute watching TV
- 8 calories per minute jumping rope

If you eat an apple that has 60 calories, how long will it take to use up the calories?				
60 calories	÷	½ calorie per minute sleeping	=	120 minutes
60 calories	÷	1 calorie per minute watching TV	=	60 minutes
60 calories	÷	8 calories per minute jumping rope	=	7½ minutes

Ways to Be Active

There are so many ways to be active. Choose activities you enjoy.

- team sports
- biking
- hiking
- dancing
- jumping rope
- walking to school
- washing the car
- skateboarding
- roller blading
- marching band
- swimming
- fencing
- badminton
- catch with your dog
- walking around a museum
- playing on jungle gyms
- walking up and down stairs
- cleaning around the house
- helping around the garden
- hopscotch
- bowling
- Frisbee
- karate
- tag

The list goes on and on!

Your heart beats about 100,000 times a day. It slows down when you're sleeping but never stops beating.

Benefits of Being Active

- makes your lungs strong so you can breathe easier and more efficiently
- helps keep arteries and veins clear for blood to flow
- makes you flexible so you can bend and stretch without injuring yourself
- helps you relax and have a restful sleep
- helps to improve your ability at sports
- gives you more energy to keep going
- helps you feel good about yourself
- makes your heart strong
- makes your bones strong
- helps control your weight
- helps prevent illness
- helps you to think
- it's fun

Warm Up Your Muscles

It's a good idea to stretch your muscles and get your heart pumping before you engage in strenuous physical activities. This helps prevent injury. Your physical education teacher or coach can teach you how to warm up correctly. For example, a fast walk before you start a long jog helps your body get ready for the challenge ahead.

"Every strike brings me closer to the next home run."
—Babe Ruth, Hall of Fame Baseball Player

Why do you sweat?
You sweat to keep your body cool. Sweating controls the temperature of your body, acting like a natural air conditioner.

What is dehydration?
Dehydration is when your body overheats from lack of water. You feel dizzy and might even faint. It can happen when you don't drink enough water, especially when you're active or when it's hot outside. It's important to drink before and after physical activities.

Set a goal!
If you're overweight, set a goal to be active. Ask your doctor and parents for help and advice. As you begin to lose weight, you'll have more energy to do the things you like to do. Be patient and feel good about your accomplishments. Every positive step you make counts!

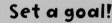

33

YOU'RE GETTING SLEEPY: THE IMPORTANCE OF SLEEP

Sleep is as important to the body as eating right and being active. Your body and brain need time to recharge to stay fit. Lack of sleep can make it harder for your body to grow and fight off illness. Studies have found that lack of sleep can be linked to being overweight, as well as to diabetes and heart disease.

Good Sleep Habits

- Try to get 10 to 11 hours of sleep each night. You'll wake up feeling energized for the busy day ahead.
- Try to go to bed at the same time every night. A routine helps your body fall asleep.
- Do something calming before bed, such as taking a bath or reading a book—it will help you relax.
- It's best not to watch a scary movie or action-packed show before bedtime. This can make it harder for you to fall asleep.
- Turn off the TV and computer screens. The moving lights make it hard for your eyes to relax.
- Don't eat foods such as chocolate or coffee ice cream, or drink soda before bedtime. These foods contain caffeine, which peps you up.
- It's a good idea to avoid snacking right before bed.

People sleep through about one third of their lives.

Gorillas go to sleep around 6:00 PM.

Most people spend about six years of their lives dreaming.

Cats can sleep up to eighteen hours a day.

MOOD FOOD: SELF-ESTEEM

Self-esteem is how you feel about yourself. When you don't feel very special, you have low self-esteem.

Many things can contribute to low self-esteem, including how you feel about your body. You may wish you were thinner or taller. It's normal to have these thoughts; everyone does. The secret to feeling better is to focus on the things you like about yourself—the things that make you special. Remember, there is no "right" body type. Healthy bodies come in all shapes and sizes. Knowing you're special and worthy of love helps keep you happy and healthy!

Laughter can make you feel happy, too! How many times have you laughed out loud and it made you feel good? Laughter is the best medicine!

FUN HOUSE

When is a cucumber like a strawberry?

When one is in a pickle and the other is in a jam.

What do bananas do best in gymnastics?

The splits!

What is a ghost's favorite fruit?

Boo-berries!

What did the baby corn say to the momma corn?

Where's pop-corn?

Ways to Improve Self-Esteem

- Think of three good things about yourself each day.
- Discover what you're good at by trying new things.
- Be kind to others—it makes you feel good about yourself.
- Treat your body with respect with healthy eating habits and an active lifestyle.
- When you fail, focus on what you learned and feel proud for trying.
- Compliment others on their accomplishments.

Depression

Depression is when you feel sad a lot. It's normal to feel sad sometimes, but if you feel sad most of the time, talk to someone you trust, such as a trusted parent or teacher. You deserve to feel good on the inside, too!

Teasing

Teasing people about their weight is uncool. It could make a person depressed and lead to low self-esteem or, in some serious cases, an eating disorder. Kids who tease often do it because they have low self-esteem themselves.

**Knock knock!
Who's there?
Lettuce!
Lettuce who?
Lettuce in and
we'll tell you!**

"By swallowing evil words unsaid, no one has ever harmed his stomach."—Winston Churchill, former British Prime Minister

WEBSITES: CHECK 'EM OUT

GENERAL HEALTH

KidsHealth
www.kidshealth.org/kid/index.jsp
Answers to questions on kids' health, including good nutrition, exercise, illnesses, smoking/alcohol/drugs, emotions, and more. (English and Spanish)

It's My Life
www.pbskids.org/itsmylife/
Answers to questions about self-esteem, eating disorders, sports, smoking/drugs, and more. Includes interviews with celebrities.

BAM! Body and Mind
www.bam.gov
Covers topics important to kids, such as fitness, peer pressure, nutrition, and more.

NUTRITION

Nutrition Explorations
www.nutritionexplorations.org/kids/
Offers nutrition information, activities, contests, and recipes.

Smart-Mouth
www.cspinet.org/smartmouth/
Offers nutrition information, recipes, video clips, and games.

FOOD PYRAMID

The U.S. Department of Agriculture
www.mypyramid.gov/kids/index.html
Offers a step-by-step explanation of the food pyramid with an interactive computer game, worksheets, poster, and coloring page.

FOOD SAFETY

The U.S. Department of Agriculture
www.fsis.usda.gov/food_safety_education/thermy_for_kids/
    index.asp
Offers tips and activities on food safety.

EXERCISE

The President's Council on Physical Fitness and Sports
www.fitness.gov
Offers information on physical fitness. You can sign up to participate in a fitness program called The President's Challenge to earn awards.

ALLERGIES

Food Allergy News for Kids
www.fankids.org/FANKid/kidindex.html
Answers to questions about allergies. Includes activities and a place to share stories, jokes, and recipes with other kids with allergies.

TEETH

American Dental Association
www.ada.org/public/games/index.asp
Shows how to brush your teeth and what to expect at the dentist's office.

SMOKING

National Center for Chronic Disease Prevention and Health Promotion
www.cdc.gov/tobacco
Gives kids the real facts about smoking and how to quit. Includes interviews with celebrities and kids.

ALCOHOL

The Cool Spot
www.thecoolspot.gov
Answers to questions about alcohol and dealing with peer pressure.

Visit
www.edmiller.com
for additional books
by Edward Miller